Edinburgh
and the Lothians
in the 1950s

With contributions by

John McLellan, Editor, *Edinburgh Evening News*
Stuart Farquhar, Special Reports, The Scotsman Publications Ltd
Gabe Stewart, Special Reports, The Scotsman Publications Ltd

With thanks to

Craig Nelson, Library Manager, The Scotsman Publications Ltd

First published in 2008 by
At Heart Ltd
32 Stamford Street
·Altrincham
Cheshire
·WA14 1EY

in conjunction with
The Scotsman Publications Ltd
108 Holyrood Road
Edinburgh
EH8 8AS

The photographs in this book have been selected from the archives of *The Scotsman*, *The Weekly Scotsman*, *Edinburgh Evening News* and *Edinburgh Evening Dispatch*.

The Weekly Scotsman ceased publication in June 1967.

The Evening News and *Evening Dispatch* merged in 1963 to become the *Evening News and Dispatch* until the *Dispatch* name was dropped in 1967.

ISBN: 978-1-84547-207-8

Printed and bound by Ashford Colour Press, Gosport.

Contents

Foreword

Looking through this fascinating selection of photographs from the archives of The Scotsman publications, it is remarkable to remember that the most recent picture was taken 49 years ago; remarkable because, by comparison with other British cities, so much has survived.

Of course Edinburgh didn't come through the town planning nightmare of the Sixties unscathed, but the vast majority of the images in this book will be instantly recognisable by Edinburgh people of all ages.

Some sights have gone, most notably Portobello's open-air pool, which in this age of global warming might have enjoyed a new lease of life, university buildings have disfigured beautiful George Square and a worthy replacement for the Waverley Market has never been found. So too were the slum tenements of St Leonard's, Dumbiedykes and Greenside swept away, but we will never know if renovation would have been a better solution than demolition and the break-up of the communities they housed.

What this book really illustrates is that by and large, the dramatic backdrop of this city has remained a constant throughout the latter half of the 20th century and while Edinburgh has not stood still and more changes are on the way, it retains all the characteristics that have kept it at the top of Europe's league of tourist destinations.

But like everywhere else, Edinburgh is a very different place socially, perhaps to be seen at its most stark in the chapter on the city's places of work. You will not see pictures of

The outdoor pool at Portobello was a great favourite with generations of Edinburgh children.

the banks or insurance companies, then proud but provincial institutions still to become the national players we know today, but of long-gone manufacturers, the absence of

Massed bands and troops at the finale of the 1954 Tattoo.

which would have been unthinkable back in the 50s.

Duncan's chocolate, Golden Wonder crisps, Walls Ice Cream and a long list of brewers dominated the world of work where now their place has largely been taken by two-bedroom flats. The North British Rubber Company, Rob Caledon shipbuilders and the Lothian deep coal mines are all now the preserve of social historians.

And the old Edinburgh Evening Dispatch, once the rival of the Evening News and which lives on today through the Dispatch amateur team golf trophy, finally disappeared in 1963 but is remembered in these pages in one of the clearest and most amusing signs of social change. Its "Housewives demonstration service", shown here in the culture chapter, was not a facility for husbands-to-be, but a show of domestic appliances. Apparently men didn't use such devices as washing machines in those days, and how times have changed...or have they?

It was also an era of mass turnouts for events large and small. Crowds thronged outside Thomson's department store to see Santa climb a golden ladder in 1955, the thousands who packed The Mound for the 1951 Gathering of the Clans dwarfed Edinburgh's Hogmanay 50 years on, and it was standing room only on Porty beach when the sun came out. More innocent times maybe, but they were communal experiences the likes of which are hard to repeat today.

The times may well still be a-changing, but as you will see from these pictures, the essence of Edinburgh's atmosphere is as unaltered as Arthur's Seat.

John McLellan
Editor, Edinburgh Evening News

In and Around Edinburgh

Acts of God have had their fair share of impact on this city. Cowgate looks less built up and congested in the 1950s, but this image is also a sad reminder of how much of its impressive architecture was swept away with the fires of 2000. Forty-five years earlier, in 1955, two fires elsewhere in the capital blazed within 24 hours of each other: one at the CW Carr warehouse and James Aitman shoe factory in Jeffrey Street; the other at the C&A Modes store on Princes Street.

Other forces of nature have similarly proved a challenge to Edinburgh citizens. Terrible floods affected the city in 1953, and freezing conditions brought the snowploughs out in force a couple of years later. But given a hot sunny day in Edinburgh, the public will still rush to the beach in droves as the picture of Cramond Beach on page 20 shows.

Pipers lead the crowds down The Mound prior to the Gathering of the Clans at Murrayfield during the Festival of Britain in 1951.

And the temptation of a bargain still brings out crowds of shoppers. Sales hunters at Grant's department store on North Bridge in July 1959 had the added thrill of seeing the shop's first escalator.

One side of human behaviour which has diminished, thanks to the rise of technology, is the political hustings. It would be a brave politician today who would face the public as Independent Liberal Sir Andrew Murray did at the foot of Leith Walk in the 1955 General Election. Whether a candidate would be more wounded by the public's indifference or indolence is hard to tell.

Crowds outside Patrick Thomson's department store on North Bridge look on as Santa Claus climbs down a golden ladder in November 1955. The shop advertised itself as 'The Store of a Thousand Gifts'.

Today, Edinburgh Castle is floodlit every night, but it was more unusual in 1953 when it was floodlit for two days to mark the rugby international between Scotland and Ireland. This photograph was taken from the steps of the Vennel.

To combat parking problems on Cockburn Street, Edinburgh police imposed a time limit of five minutes. The Clinkscales, Oswald & Sons shop front is visible at the top of Fleshmarket Close.

Taken from Tron Kirk spire, a view of the Royal Mile from the High Street to the Castle, with St Giles' Cathedral on the left.

Looking up St Mary's Street at the junction with the Cowgate, Holyrood Road and Pleasance. The buildings at the bottom left have since been demolished, and a hotel now stands on the site.

Aerial view of George Square, with original buildings intact on the east, south and west sides. The majority of these buildings were soon to be demolished to make way for new buildings for the University of Edinburgh.

The view from an Edinburgh Castle window, looking south-east over the Grassmarket to Arthur's Seat.

Aerial view, looking towards Edinburgh Castle and Arthur's Seat. In the foreground is Princes Street Station, which closed in 1965.

'Parking pandemonium' in George Street in 1959. Some things never change!

The statue of Greyfriars Bobby is replaced on its pedestal following repairs that were required after it was knocked over by a car in June 1954.

Looking down Leith Street towards Picardy Place. Picture shows the Top Deck restaurant, John Collier menswear and Timpson's shoe shop.

Snow and slush at a tram stop in Edinburgh, looking north down Lothian Road to the West End in February 1955.

The Royal Scots Greys march up the Royal Mile towards Edinburgh
Castle, as part of Queen Elizabeth II and Prince Philip, Duke of
Edinburgh's visit to the city during their tour of Scotland in July 1956.

Portobello High Street. The building with the clock is the Old Town Hall, which in 1953 was a public library. Today it is Portobello Police Station.

Young rowers on the Union Canal between Gilmore Place and Fountainbridge, looking towards the canal terminus.

Boys in canoes on the Union Canal at Viewforth in 1957, with the lift bridge in the background. The North British Rubber Company, Castle Mills, (pictured left) has now been demolished.

The bridge in Dean Village, with Holy Trinity Church in the background.

Colinton Parish Church in the winter sunshine in 1953.

A soldier standing guard outside Leith Fort on the day its closure was announced. First built in 1779 to protect Leith, the Fort had housed prisoners of the Napoleonic Wars and had been an army base until 1955. The site is now a housing development, though some remnants of the fort survive.

Top left: New road markings were laid out on Lothian Road in 1957. Although they were designed to help traffic flow more easily, motorists were not convinced, and the police had to issue a statement through the press urging drivers to follow the arrows.

Top right: Cramond Brig photographed from Queensferry Road.

Above: Aerial view of the Restalrig area of Edinburgh, with the Munrospun knitting factory in the foreground.

Holidaymakers at Cramond beach.

Shops on St John's Road in Corstorphine in 1959.

Gorgie Road's shops, here pictured with the awnings down. Behind is Tynecastle Park, home of Heart of Midlothian FC.

Shops in the Churchill area of Morningside Road in 1959.

Bailie James Campbell posts the first letter after the unveiling of the new Post Office pillar box, bearing the insignia of Queen Elizabeth II in November 1952. This postbox in The Inch in Edinburgh was the first in Scotland to show the new insignia.

A snow plough at work in Newington Road, Edinburgh.

Torrential rain during a thunderstorm in July 1953 took just 15 minutes to cause flood damage. Here, a bus ploughs through the water under Slateford Railway Bridge.

Workmen repairing damage in Princes Street Gardens caused by the floods.

Disruption on London Road
in June 1955 as workmen pull
up the road to remove the
tram lines.

During the 1955 general
election campaign,
Independent Liberal
candidate Sir Andrew Murray
addresses people at an open
air meeting by the Queen
Victoria statue at the foot of
Leith Walk.

A lollipop man helps primary school children cross the street in Morningside after the school bell rings in 1954.

Pipers lead the crowds down The Mound prior to the Gathering of the Clans at Murrayfield during the Festival of Britain in 1951.

As part of the Festival of Britain in 1951 a Gathering of the Clans was held in Edinburgh. Here, vast crowds follow as pipers parade down Princes Street and the mound.

Lantern street decorations in Princes Street for the 1959 Edinburgh Festival.

The Edinburgh City Police Pipe Band marches along Princes Street during the 1959 Edinburgh Festival. In the foreground is a maypole that was erected for the Festival.

1955 saw not one, but two spectacular fires occuring in Edinburgh within 24 hours of each other. The first was a fire at the C.W. Carr warehouse and James Aitman shoe factory in Jeffrey Street, followed by a devastating blaze at the C & A Modes store in Princes Street the next day. A fire engine with extended ladder is pictured at the scene of the first fire.

Firemen on turntable ladders fight the blaze on Princes Street.

View from the North British Hotel on Princes Street, now the Balmoral. The area at the bottom was the roof of the Waverley Market, and is now the site of Princes Mall shopping centre.

It may have been the 1950s, but Edinburgh did not escape traffic jams. This tram congestion at the West End of Princes Street was caused by roadworks.

View of Princes Street, Princes Street Gardens and the Scott Monument, taken from the spire of Tron Kirk.

Miss M. Currie gives one of the stuffed bears a brush up on the balcony of Marcus, a furriers on Princes Street in 1958.

Junction of Princes Street and Queensferry Street. In 1953 it was announced that Vallance the Confectioner had been sold and was to become Rankins fruit shop. Above it is the sign for Aitken and Niven outfitters.

Snow falls on the West End of
Princes Street with St John's
church and St Cuthbert's church
in the foreground, and the
frontage of the Caledonian Hotel
to the right. Edinburgh Castle is
pictured in the background.

A queue of trams on Princes
Street after an overhead bracing
broke at The Mound in November
1952. Engineers had the trams
moving again within 40 minutes.

Gardeners lay out the 1959 Floral Clock in West Princes Street Gardens.
The clock commemorated the bicentenary of Robert Burns' birth.

The 1953 Floral Clock in Princes Street Gardens. The design spells out Elizabeth Regina in honour of the Queen's coronation and her forthcoming State visit to the city.

Penguins from Edinburgh Zoo entertain the crowds at the Ross Bandstand in Princes Street Gardens.

Girls feeding the pigeons in Princes Street Gardens in the spring of 1954.

Crowds of holidaymakers watch a session of open-air
dancing at the Ross Bandstand in Princes Street Gardens.

A February blizzard leaves a blanket of snow over Princes Street Gardens.

Top left: In November 1959, a Corporation Planning meeting heard that in this tenement in Nicholson Street 'floors tilt crazily, doors are askew, windows jam and five families have to share one sink'.

Top right: In an attempt to highlight problems faced by property owners in Edinburgh, the owner of this dilapidated tenement in Beaumont Place, St Leonards, offered to sell it to an MP for a penny. The MP, William Reid, had spoken out against rent increases.

Above: Councillors Pat Rogan and Norman McQueen visit the houses in Holyrood Square, off Holyrood Road, to announce to residents who were living in 'squalid conditions' that they were to be rehoused within 18 months.

As part of the redevelopment of Edinburgh's deprived areas, one of the first streets to be demolished was Arthur Street, Pleasance.

Housing in Edinburgh in the 1950s. The headline that went with this photograph was 'This is Scotland's disgrace'. This picture is taken from Heriot Mount beside James Clark's School, looking towards Dumbiedykes Road (right), St Leonards Hill (left) and Carnegie Street (straight ahead). All were demolished within a few years.

In December 1959 Edinburgh
councillors toured the city
slums in the St Leonards area.
The slums were demolished in
the early 1960s.

A resident of Prospect Place
shouts at councillors touring
the St Leonards slums in
December 1959.

Greenside Row, off Leith Street, in 1959. These were described by the City's Medical Officer as the 'city's worst slums' at an inquiry to discuss their proposed demolition.

Customers enjoy a rummage at the half-yearly sale at
Patrick Thomson's department store in North Bridge.

Wrapped up against the early morning cold, these intrepid bargain hunters are first in the queue at Blyth's department store in Earl Grey Street for the start of the January sale.

People made special trips to the new extension at
Grant's department store on North Bridge to use the first
escalator in Edinburgh, which was installed in July 1959.

The opening of Marks & Spencer's Princes Street store in 1957,
their first branch in Edinburgh. This picture shows the Ladieswear
department, with rows of summer dresses priced at 37s 6d.

Singer Gracie Fields visits the Television Lounge in Jenners Department Store. The other ladies are her friends Mrs Mary Davey and Miss Greta Beattie.

The opening of Greens, a new hairdressing salon on Castle Street, in March 1959.

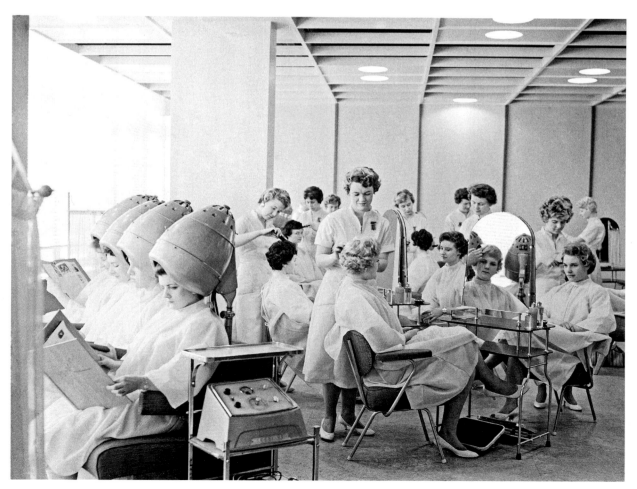

Staff and pupils of Murrayburn Primary School at the children's leaving party in the school hall.

Concentration is key for the egg and spoon race during sports day at George Watson's Ladies College.

The grocery section of J. & R. Allan's new food store on South Bridge, which opened on 1 December 1954.

High spirits as school ends for the summer holidays and the race is on to get the summer started.

Problems are set for the teachers of St Cuthbert's School in February 1952, with ten sets of twins on the school register, pictured here with teacher Mr H Bocker.

Top left: In 1956 the tiered classrooms like this one at South Morningside School were beginning to be phased out.

Top right: Children put their chairs on their desks after their first day at John Watson's School in Belford Road. The building now houses the Scottish National Gallery of Modern Art.

Above: Children eating school meals in Edinburgh's smallest school on Peffermill Road. The old tin school was used as an annexe for St Francis Primary School in Craigmillar.

Out and About in the Lothians

Photographs of the capital's rural outskirts in the 1950s present a real contrast: examples of dramatic change stand alongside illustrations of the timeless nature of the countryside and its traditions.

So many architectural features in these images of the past seem comfortingly familiar, even if the cars' designs and ladies' fashions are dated. Similarly, traditional community events such as festivals and ridings still serve their purpose in bringing people together in common celebration. Many Lothian towns may feel increasingly like dormitory towns for capital commuters, but each one's proud heritage is often still energetically maintained by traditional celebrations that bring out a sense of communal pride in everyone.

A view of Lasswade, Midlothian, looking towards the Pentland Hills.

Some change is beneath the surface. For example, the Lady Victoria Colliery in Newtongrange has now morphed into the Scottish Mining Museum. And the introduction in 1953 of a one-way system certainly helped ease the bottleneck in the High Street, Dalkeith without altering a great deal of its character. In contrast, Loanhead's Clerk Street has completely changed, and is now built up with shops and busy with traffic.

Finally there are those images that seem to step out of pure fantasy. Those who ever experienced Dunbar's outdoor swimming pool before its closure in the 1980s will either remember it with fondness, or a wee shiver, or perhaps both. Everyone else is likely to stare in amazement at the wondrous image on page 63. Here, the austere beauty of a natural backdrop of sheer rock faces, looming out from the sea, together with the remains of Dunbar Castle overlooking the splendid scene, is strangely at odds with the carefree fun and laughter of children frolicking in the water. Happy days indeed.

Snow on the River Almond at Livingston Village.

The Lady Victoria Colliery in Newtongrange. It is now the site of the Scottish Mining Museum.

View from the tower of the High Church at Bathgate, West Lothian, looking down Mid Street from its junction with Hopetoun Street.

A bus stops at traffic lights on the High Street, Dalkeith. It was announced in 1953 that a one-way system was to be introduced to ease the bottleneck in the High Street.

North Berwick, East Lothian, as seen from the beach on the East Links golf course.

Looking along Clerk Street, the main thoroughfare in Loanhead, Midlothian.

The High Street in Dunbar, East Lothian, in 1959.

Crowning ceremony for the 1955 Bo'ness Fair Queen, Margaret Grant.

The traditional Fishermen's Walk in Musselburgh sees
the fishwives and children parading through the streets.

The Riding of the Marches procession in Linlithgow. The winning float was owned by Aitken's.

Musselburgh's Honest Lad, Robert Morgan and his Lass, Betty Russell, wave to watching crowds as they push out from the shore during the Harbour Ceremony at the 1959 Musselburgh Festival.

Fishing boats in the harbour
at Cockenzie in East Lothian.

The remains of Dunbar Castle, East Lothian, overlooking the outdoor swimming pool which closed in the 1980s.

At Work

Over the last half century, the world of work, whether in the mines or the breweries, the office or factory, has changed beyond imagination. So much of the Lothians' heavy industry has evaporated, it seems almost surreal that men once worked day after day digging underground in Penkaet, East Lothian, known as the 'coal mine in the woods'.

Machines have transformed the working lives of both men and women, making boring repetitive tasks such as packing foodstuffs a thing of the past. Of course some things never change – fishermen still unload their catches, although traders no longer unload fruit and veg at the aptly named Market Street.

The men take a break in the Scottish Oil Roman Camp Works at Broxburn, West Lothian. The works were in need of extensive repair and closed down in 1956.

Among the capital's more unusual light industry to be found in Edinburgh 50 years ago was Walls Ice Cream factory in Craigmillar and Adolph Teurer's wig factory in Canonmills. In 1959 Leith wine and spirits merchants, J.G. Thomson and Co Ltd celebrated their 250th anniversary. Nearly 25 years later, in 1983, the Vaults complex was sold to a consortium including the actor Russell Hunter, to provide premises for the nascent Scotch Malt Whisky Society Ltd, which still promotes the amber nectar today.

Edinburgh's largest factory in the 1950s, the North British Rubber Company's works at Castle Mills, employed nearly 3,700 people making Wellingtons, golf balls, flooring, tyres and hot water bottles. It closed in 1973.

Workmen rolling barrels at Drybrough's Brewery in Craigmillar. The brewery closed in 1987, and the site was subsequently demolished, to be replaced by flats.

Miners come up from the pit for midday break at the Penkaet coal mine, Pencaitland, East Lothian. Owned at the time by the Gordon family, it was known as 'the coal mine in the woods'.

Temporary staff were employed by the Post Office to help during the Christmas rush. Here, cards and letters are being sorted in the primary sorting office.

Workers pack crisps in polythene bags at the newly opened Golden Wonder crisp factory at Sighthill in 1958.

Top left: McVitie & Price cake and biscuit factory in Gorgie. Forewoman, Mrs Jean Penhaligon, watches Miss Maureen Russell and Miss Margaret Kaye pick out rows of biscuits for packing.

Top right: Women at work in George Waugh's haggis factory in Edinburgh. Pictured left is Georgette Gray, a portrait painter originally from the Channel Islands who took a job at the factory to provide a steady income.

Above: Packing chocolates at Duncan's confectionery factory in Edinburgh.

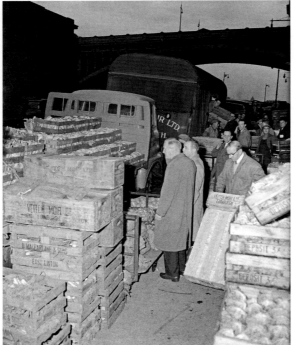

Fishermen, who would be in-shore herring fishing on the Firth of Forth during the winter months, unload their catch at Newhaven Harbour.

Traders unload their stock at the fruit and vegetable market on Edinburgh's Market Street in 1959.

During the printing unions' strike in 1959, four men on early picket duty while away the time with a game of dominoes outside A.B. Fleming & Co ink factory, Caroline Park Works, Granton.

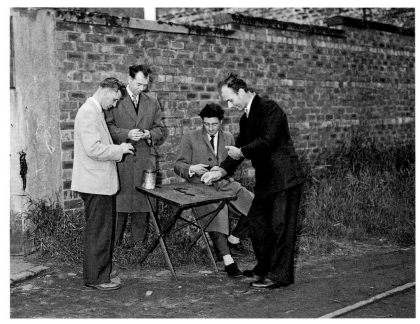

Mr F. Mackenzie is wrapped up well to work in the storage room of the Walls Ice Cream factory in Craigmillar.

A woman washes blankets in Liddells Laundry on Beaverhall Road, Edinburgh, in 1952.

A new electrically operated dustcart at work in Edinburgh. St Stephen's Church can be seen in the background.

Park-keepers in the Queen's Park were issued with scooters
in 1956. Thomas Wilson patrols on his scooter next to St
Margaret's Loch with St Anthony's Chapel in the background.

The Mound proved so hazardous to drivers in bad weather that in 1959
it was decided to lay an 'electric blanket' under the tarmac. Pictured are
engineers with two different types of mesh and wiring which were used
in an experiment before one was chosen and laid under the tarmac. The
scheme proved less than satisfactory and a few years later was unplugged.

Workmen on the scaffolding for the construction of the Edinburgh University Medical School extension in George Square.

Delivery boys are swamped under Christmas
poultry, trees and parcels in the last-minute rush
at the Edinburgh Corporation's Shrubhill depot.

In 1951 Edinburgh's largest factory was the North British Rubber Company's works at Castle Mills, which employed 3,664 people. The company was founded in 1856 by Henry Lee Norris who wanted to produce rubber wellington boots. They also produced golf balls, flooring, tyres and hot water bottles. During the First World War the mills worked day and night to produce over 1 million pairs of boots. The company changed its name to Uniroyal in 1966, and finally the factory closed in 1973. Here, hot water bottles are being given a final polish before getting sent out.

Staff running out of the factory at the end of the shift.

Still making wellington boots after almost a century.

Sally the elephant lifts her keeper up with her trunk at Edinburgh Zoo in 1952.

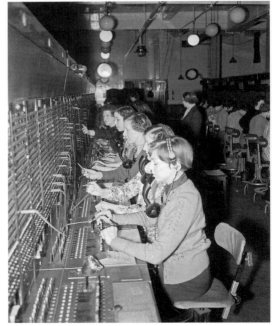

Five members of the Edinburgh Telephone Choir at work at the telephone exchange on Rose Street. They manually connected all the telephone lines at the switchboard. From front: Miss Lawson, Miss Millar, Miss Cherrie, Miss Snowdon and Mrs Brown.

Gulls circle in search for food as the crew of the Golden Effort clean their nets at Newhaven following a night of sprat fishing.

A wig takes shape under a worker's hands at the Adolph Teurer Factory in Canonmills, Edinburgh.

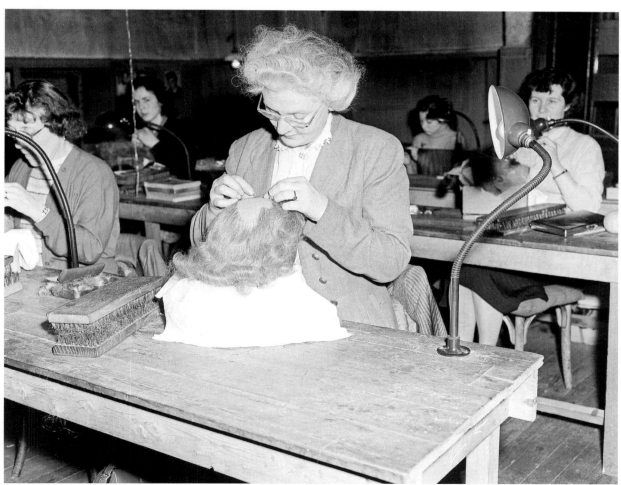

In 1959, Leith wine and spirits merchants, J.G.Thomson and Co Ltd, celebrated their 250th anniversary. Here, works manager Mr W L Henderson checks a sample of wine using a candle in The Vaults. Part of The Vaults has now been converted into flats, while the Scotch Malt Whisky Society is resident in another.

John Barnyard and Margaret Cook, a young milkman and paper girl, meet on their early morning rounds in October 1959. John is showing off the new broadsheet sized *Evening Dispatch*. The *Dispatch* would later merge with the *Edinburgh Evening News* in 1963.

Firemen of Lauriston Station in Edinburgh practicing on a 100ft ladder.

Recruiting sergeant Mrs A H Hume shows staff from Binns department store, Edinburgh, where to sign on as voluntary helpers in Edinburgh's Tuberculosis X-ray Campaign. Mr M G Nicol is first in the queue.

Firemen spray their hoses over the roof of a blazing warehouse belonging to theatrical costumiers William Mutrie & Son on Bells Brae, Dean Village in May 1957.

Motorcycle police advising a motorist in 1954.

Mounted police out for morning exercise pass by Campbell's Argyle Brewery in the Cowgate. The brewery site is now student accommodation.

Transport

Few areas have seen more change over the last 50 years than transportation. The 1950s was an era of firsts and lasts in Edinburgh: the introduction of the first double decker buses; the last horse-drawn taxi; the momentous building of the Forth Road Bridge in 1958, which opened in 1964. And, of course, some vehicles have come full circle. Among those many thousands of people who lined the route of the last tram, No.28, on 16 November 1956, few could have imagined trams would be reintroduced half a century later.

Fifty years ago, car drivers may not have had to experience the interminable Forth Road Bridge queues, but their patience was equally tested as they waited to cross the Firth by ferry. Similarly, in the 1950s, holidaymakers may not have crammed airline check-in desks, but they came in droves to St Andrew Square, lining up for buses to take them on their Trades holiday.

Cars queue at South Queensferry to board the ferry across the Forth, in the days before the Forth Road Bridge.

This was the era that saw the birth of the commuter, travelling further afield from home to work, even if the new 'businessman's express' train, which took 6 hours 40 minutes to run from Edinburgh to London, seems a crawl today. But all work and no play would have made Jock a dull boy, and the introduction of special trains to Glasgow meant more football fans could travel to more games.

Transport was no longer just a means of getting from A to B, but a lifestyle choice. From Austin Metropolitans and Triumphs to Minis, as private ownership of vehicles increased, so too did their social value. A vehicle became an extension of its owner's character and personality. Vespa Club members' choice of scooter said something about them. And as like-minded people, it seemed only natural they would socialise together.

A Washington Bomber flies
over the large crowds attending
the Battle of Britain Day
air display at Turnhouse, in
September 1952. The large
aircraft is a Hastings of
Transport Command.

Passengers wait their turn
to embark in the new
Turnhouse terminal building
at Edinburgh Airport.

Jill Morgan, an air hostess with BEA (British European Airways), stands on the steps to the plane at Turnhouse airport.

The maiden flight of the short-lived Hythe flying boat *Hudson* service from Southampton to Leith. The plane arrives at Leith Docks carrying 26 passengers, guests of operators Aquila Airways Ltd.

An Austin Metropolitan car with Fettes College in the background.

The first Triumph Herald in Edinburgh is shown at a private preview
in the showrooms of Messrs Rossleigh Ltd of Shandwick Place.

Cars at the Ford motor show in Waverley Market, staged by Alexanders of Edinburgh.

A new Mini Minor draws a lot of attention on Princes Street. The driver is model Marion Wyllie who was about to drive the car to the Concours d'Elegance at the Royal Scottish Automobile Club's Festival.

Agents from around the Lothians admire the new Morris Oxford at Westfield, Edinburgh.

In 1952 Edinburgh's only horse-drawn taxi conveyed visitors from the Castle to the Palace of Holyroodhouse.

Sergeant Robb of the
AA Road Service
affixes a diversion
road sign in position.

An ambulance crew
prepare to set out from
their headquarters
in Lochrin Place,
Edinburgh in 1958.

Aerial view showing the
progress of the construction
of the Forth Road Bridge
in 1959. The bridge opened
five years later.

A painter walking down the centre girder of the Forth Bridge looks across to the ferry pier and the North Queensferry workings of the new Forth Road Bridge, which opened in 1964.

The *Sir William Wallace* approaches the Fife side of the Forth, passing the southbound ferry pictured in the foreground.

Members of the Edinburgh Vespa Club gather for a social evening in Free Gardeners Hall in 1959.

Queues at Edinburgh Bus Station, off St Andrew Square, as the Trades holiday rush begins.

Edinburgh's latest double decker bus is examined by a driver and a conductor at Shrubhill depot. The bus was one of 60 that were bought from London and reconditioned and rebodied.

The bus conductor tries out the bell push in a new bus.

Below left: Thousands of people lined the street to bid farewell to the trams on 16 November 1956, the last day they ran in Edinburgh.

Below right: Mr R Crawford collects fares on the last No.28 tram.

Right: Souvenir hunters search for pennies bent by the last tram.

Hibs fans queue at Edinburgh's Princes Street station (also known as Caledonian station) for the special train to Glasgow in March 1959. Their trip was to end in disappointment though, as the Scottish Cup tie ended in a 2-1 win for Third Lanark.

Twelve passengers were hurt when the Dundee–Edinburgh train crashed into the buffers at Waverley Station in March 1958.

People queuing at Waverley Station during a bus strike in July 1957.

The new *Talisman* express train passing through Portobello Station on its first run from Edinburgh to London. Described as a 'businessman's express' it covered the journey in 6 hours 40 minutes.

Arts, Entertainment and Culture

As the availability of leisure time in the 1950s rocketed, so did the cult of the celebrity. Plenty made their way to the capital. Singers who hit the high notes here included Cliff Richard, Johnnie Ray, Paul Robeson, George Formby, Shirley Bassey, Maria Callas and Mario Lanza. American stars in Edinburgh's spotlight included actor Clayton Moore, aka the Lone Ranger, and Roy Rogers, Dale Evans and Trigger. Gene Kelly, Bob Hope, Danny Kaye and Laurel and Hardy also entertained the capital, while local lads Jackie Dennis (remember Purple People Eater?) and Sean Connery began to hit the big time.

The various festivals caught the attention of the world and so began Edinburgh's love affair with international culture. Ballet dancer Margot Fonteyn attended the Homage to Diaghilev exhibition in 1954. Claire Bloom, Richard Burton and Fay Compton starred in an Old Vic production of *Hamlet* in 1953. Five years later Jimmy Logan and Jack Radcliffe performed their own version of the classic at the King's Theatre.

American actress Vera-Ellen leads a pipe band in Princes Street while filming the 1956 movie *Let's Be Happy*.

During the decade, the Film Festival came into its own, attracting the likes of Orson Welles and Dirk Bogarde and the city of Edinburgh itself played a starring role in Fifties' films such as *Let's Be Happy*, in which American actress Vera-Ellen led a pipe band down Princes Street; and *The 39 Steps*, starring Kenneth More, which included scenes shot on the Forth Bridge.

The Military Tattoo, which perhaps epitomises the antithesis of celebrity, was as spectacular event then as it is now.

This was also a decade that saw a continuation of the changing role of women, which would impact on everything from fashion and beauty to cookery and child care.

Singer Cliff Richard strikes a pose backstage at The Usher Hall in Edinburgh in 1959. Reports of the concert describe it as 'sheer bedlam' as Cliff, in a shocking pink jacket, thrilled 5,000 fans.

Roy Rogers, Dale Evans and Trigger arrive at the Caledonian Hotel in Edinburgh on 21 February 1954. They were appearing for a week at the Empire Theatre.

The Five Past Eight
Show was a lavish
variety revue. Pictured
are cast members
(from left) Peter
Butterworth, Digby
Wolfe on the violin,
and Rikki Fulton.

Jimmy Logan and
Jack Radcliffe at
the King's Theatre
in 1958 performing
their own version of
Hamlet in the Five
Past Eight Show.

Opera singer Mario Lanza enjoys his meal at the Caledonian Hotel, Edinburgh, in 1958.

Filming the Forth Bridge scenes for the *The 39 Steps*, in September 1958. Here, star of the film Kenneth More is seen to the right, pointing, while the unit director places the camera by the train tracks.

Top left: American singer Johnnie Ray autographs a picture for fan Alice Murray at the Empire Theatre, in 1955.

Top right: Sean Connery appearing in *The Seashell* at the King's Theatre, in 1959. While in the city he stayed with his parents in Fountainbridge.

Above: Actor Richard Hearne, who played children's entertainer Mr Pastry, visits Patrick Thomson's store and signs autographs for his fans.

Actor Gene Kelly, with film producer Arthur Freed, checking into the Caledonian Hotel in April 1953.

Bob Hope shows what he thinks of a poster for a Bing Crosby film at Poole's Cinema in 1952. He was in town for his first ever Edinburgh appearance at the Usher Hall.

Singer Paul Robeson arrives at the Caledonian Hotel for a concert at the Usher Hall.

George Formby is swamped by autograph hunters at the Press Ball at the Assembly Rooms in October 1956.

Scottish pop singer Jackie Dennis puts out milk bottles at his home in Broughton Road, Edinburgh. Jackie had hits with *Purple People Eater* and *La Dee Da*, played on the *Perry Como Show* in America and performed in Las Vegas, but his fame was short-lived.

The actress Diana Dors looks at donations given to the *Evening Dispatch* and Gaumont-Odeon cinema's Christmas Gifts for Sick Children appeal, in the New Victoria cinema. She was appearing in the play *Remains to be Seen* at the King's Theatre.

Singer Shirley Bassey backstage with her poodle at the Empire Theatre in September 1958.

Stan Laurel and Oliver Hardy at the Princes Street railway station, on 13 April 1954. The actors were on their way the Caledonian Hotel, where they were staying during their run at the Empire Theatre.

American comedian and actor Danny Kaye meets children at Walpole Hall in 1956 before appearing at the Regal Cinema.

Actor Clayton Moore, who played the Lone Ranger on television, visits Princess Margaret Rose Hospital in August 1958.

Craigmillar Castle provided a spectacular setting for the Oxford University Players' performance of Edward II during the Edinburgh Festival Fringe of 1954.

Otto Klemperer conducts the Philharmonia Orchestra in a programme of Beethoven for the opening concert of the 1958 Edinburgh Festival in Usher Hall.

French film stars bring a touch of glamour to the 1958 Film Festival in the Film House in Hill Street. From left: Noelle Adam, Dominique Wilms, Nicole Berger and Nadine Tallier.

Ballet dancer Margot Fonteyn attends the Homage to Diaghilev exhibition at the 1954 Edinburgh Festival.

Opera singer Maria Callas is met by Mr R Ponsonby at Turnhouse airport in August 1957. Ms Callas was appearing at the Edinburgh Festival with the opera company, La Piccola Scala, in a production of *La Sonnambula*.

Claire Bloom, Richard Burton and Fay Compton reading the Edinburgh Festival programme in August 1953. They were starring in the Old Vic production of *Hamlet*.

Actor and director Orson Welles arrives at the Cameo Cinema to give a lecture at the 1953 Edinburgh Film Festival.

Film producer Betty Box, director Ralph Thomas, and actor Dirk Bogarde read the programme for the 1955 Edinburgh Film Festival at the Film House in Hill Street.

A matinee performance of the 1952 Edinburgh Tattoo on the esplanade of Edinburgh Castle. The North British Hotel and Waverley Station can be seen in the background.

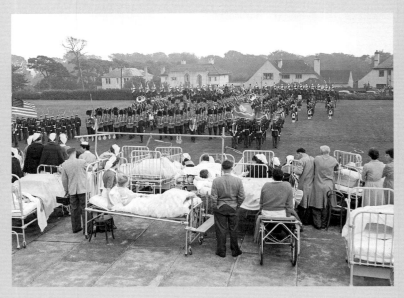

Nurses and hospital porters bring the young patients of Princess Margaret Rose Hospital outside to watch the Tattoo performers in September 1958.

Brigadier Alasdair MacLean plans the Edinburgh Tattoo for 1958, using a cardboard model of Edinburgh Castle and sets of model soldiers.

Massed pipes and drums form a figure of eight during the
1956 Edinburgh Tattoo on the esplanade of the Castle.

Top left: Three male models display summer outfits at a fashion show for men in Edinburgh's Music Hall in 1959.

Top right: Models wearing fur hats for a show by French of George Street in 1959.

Above: The Davy Crockett fashion was at its height in the Fifties, as this man in Princes Street shows.

As part of the 1956 Scottish Fashion Festival, three models in tartan visit Edinburgh Castle. The models being admired by the sentry are Pat Annan, Dorothy Reid and Candy Gilbey.

Six models pose for a fashion show for Darling's of Princes Street in 1959.

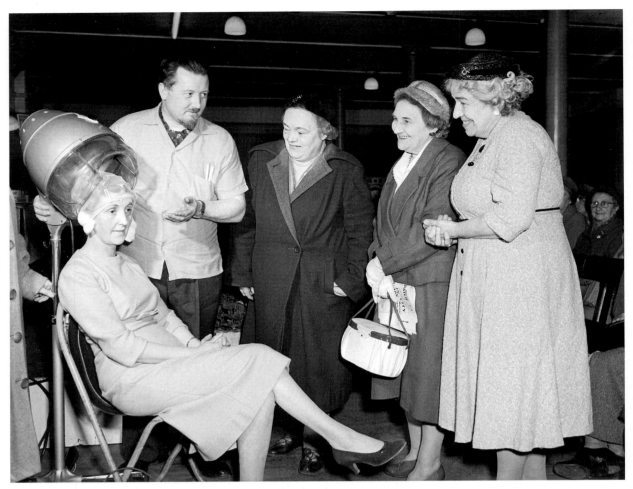

At the *Evening Dispatch* Housewives' Demonstration, Mr L H Clacy, technical adviser of Vitapointe in Paris, shows how to tint your hair.

An exhibition in Forth Street displays kitchen furniture made by disabled men at the Remploy factory in Granton.

An early visitor inspects a washing machine at the 1959 Ideal Homes Exhibition in Waverley Market.

Washing Day in Edinburgh. A T-shaped drier in Milnes Close off the High Street, with washing hung on a pulley outside the tenement window.

A demonstrator from Burco Ltd shows a washing machine in use at the Evening Dispatch Housewives' Demonstration Service at the Free Gardeners' Hall in Picardy Place.

Miss Barbara Barnes, head of Persil Home Washing bureau, demonstrates Persil washing powder.

Two women relax at a bamboo cocktail bar, complete with stools and bottle rack, from Hong Kong. It was available from Hendry Decor furniture store in July 1959.

Cowboys Douglas Currie and Jimmy Graham playing with their toy guns at The Inch in Edinburgh.

Children running down Johnston Street, in Leith. As the sign shows, the road was a designated children's playground, with vehicles banned between 4pm and sunset.

Girls playing 'Mother' in Holyrood Park. The tenements in the background on the right were soon to be demolished.

Children playing on the back green in Gorgie.

Children playing peevers (hopscotch) in Lapicide Place, Leith.

Children in Marchmont prepare for a concert on the back green in 1959.

Archers in a North Fort Street yard in Leith. Kenneth Dalzell prepares the target of tin cans, watched by Tommy Watt, George Sutherland, Jim Robertson and Archie Millar.

Hallowe'en guisers visit a night watchman at the Grassmarket in 1957.

Three boys breaking up the ice on St Margaret's Loch in the
winter of 1959, with St Anthony's Chapel in the background.

The now demolished paddling pool beside
St Margaret's Loch in Holyrood Park.

Holidaymakers at Portobello beach, Edinburgh, watch
children performing at the seaside mission in July 1954.

Dogs have a day out at the Regal Cinema, Edinburgh to see *Old Yeller* in 1958.

Usherette Joyce Hawthorne is held up by children who were members of the ABC Minor Club at the Lyceum Cinema in Slateford Road. They were dressed as cowboys to watch the film *The Law and Jake Wade*.

Three Royal Navy sailors judge the Miss Edinburgh beauty contest at the Palais de Danse.

A girl in a sack dress jives during the 1958 Edinburgh Jazz Festival in Waverley Market.

The newly refurbished Palais de Danse plays host to Mecca Bingo's 21st birthday party in November 1958. The Palais had been constructed out of the back of the picture house and in 1956 the cinema was converted into an entrance hall for the Palais, which was the largest in Britain. At that time there were 60 staff and a resident band leader, Harry Roy. The dancing was non-stop (a novelty for the time) and facilitated by a revolving stage that brought the next band around immediately. In 1957 a new dance floor was installed, built on springs.

Before today's *Strictly Come Dancing*, the competition to watch was *Come Dancing*. A BBC Television cameraman films the Edinburgh formation dancing team for the programme in the Palais de Danse in January 1958.

Cupid's Corner soft drinks bar in the newly refurbished Palais de Danse in November 1958.

The Palais de Danse's Miss Lambretta competition. The finalists pose with a motor scooter in October 1958.

The Waverley Market was used for many different exhibitions and events, including the Scottish Kennel Club Dog Show in 1958.

Gillian Bowen gives her boxer dog some encouragement before the judging at the Caledonian Canine Society's show at Waverley Market.

Sally the elephant gives children rides at Edinburgh Zoo during the Spring holiday in 1957.

The Corps de Ballet of the
Edinburgh Ballet Theatre
in their dressing room
at the Gateway Theatre
during rehearsals.

May Liddell demonstrates
the latest craze – the
hula-hoop – at the
Woodhouse's Staff Dance
in the Assembly Rooms'
Edinburgh suite.

The coffee room of the Edinburgh Festival Club in the Assembly Rooms in 1952.

Diners try out The Barbecue restaurant which opened on Forrest Road, Edinburgh, in June 1958. It is now Doctors Bar.

Generations of Edinburgh children enjoyed the outdoor pool at Portobello. The much-loved facility, which opened in 1936, ran at a financial deficit throughout the 1970s and was eventually closed down. For a number of years it lay empty before being demolished in 1988. The site currently houses a five-a-side football complex and an indoor bowling centre.

Trades holidaymakers taking to the water at Portobello beach.

Crowds of holidaymakers on Portobello Beach in May 1952 with a funfair and rollercoaster in the background.

Queen Elizabeth II and Prince Philip, Duke of Edinburgh at the 'Sunset ceremony' in July 1958 at the Palace of Holyroodhouse, which had become a traditional part of Royal Visits to Edinburgh. The Royal couple watch members of the Royal Scottish Country Dance society.

Queen Elizabeth II and the Duke of Edinburgh arrive at Queen's Park to watch a gymkhana during her Coronation visit.

The Queen Mother inspecting soldiers of the 1st Battalion Black Watch at Redford Barracks, Edinburgh. As the regiment's Colonel-in-Chief, she was paying a visit before the battalion shipped to Cyprus in 1958.

Spectators watch from on high in February 1953 as the Royal party arrives at Edinburgh Castle for the traditional ceremony of presenting the Sovereign with the key for the castle.

In a traditional ceremony on the lawn of Holyroodhouse the Queen accepts a Reddendo in the form of a brooch from the Queen's Body Guard for Scotland, the Royal Company of Archers. The Reddendo is presented by the Captain, the Duke of Buccleuch and Queensberry.

Queen Elizabeth and Prince Philip, Duke of Edinburgh attend the Royal Garden Party at Holyroodhouse during their tour of Scotland in July 1956.

The Royal Procession reaches the top of the Mound, on 24 June 1953. The Queen was making her way to St Giles' Cathedral for a service to mark the return of the Honours of Scotland (also known as the Scottish Crown Jewels) during her Coronation visit.

The slopes of Queen's Park provide a splendid view overlooking the Palace of Holyroodhouse during the Queen's inspection of Cadet organisations in 1952.

Sport

In footballing terms, the 1950s was truly a decade of two halves for Edinburgh.

Ask any Hibs fan about the Fifties and their eyes will light up. Two League title wins. The first British club to play in Europe. More than 65,000 at Easter Road. A team so joyous to watch that their 1953 South American tour is said to have influenced the Brazilians' philosophy of attacking football. The Famous Five helped Hibs dominate football in Edinburgh and beyond as the Easter Road side won titles in 1949, 1951 and 1952.

Across the city, Hearts carved out their own niche in history, winning the Scottish Cup in 1956, the League Cup three times in the space of five years, and the League in 1958 and 1960. In the early 1950s, Hearts' answer to the Famous Five was the Terrible Trio who combined power, intelligence and trickery respectively to terrify defences across the land.

Hearts fans at Hampden Park for the 1956 Scottish Cup final against Celtic.

On the golfing circuit, Muirfield was where Great Britain's triumphed over the USA to win the 1952 Curtis Cup, and where Gary Player held aloft the Claret Jug, as winner of the Open Championships in 1959.

This was the decade when Empire Games boxing gold medallist Jackie Brown was welcomed home borne aloft on the shoulders of supporters; when Edinburgh held its first ever stock car race at Meadowbank and when the Harlem Globetrotters played an exhibition match at Murrayfield Ice Rink.

Murrayfield Stadium hosted the City of Edinburgh Highland Games in 1953 and five years later, this was where Scotland's rugby team celebrated a 12-8 victory over Australia.

Boating, horseracing, cycling, and curling were all popular in Edinburgh in the 1950s. Even ski jumping came to the Braid Hills in Edinburgh in a big way in 1951, courtesy of a giant delivery of snow imported from Norway. As a result, more than 10,000 people came to Edinburgh to watch and winter sports generally benefited, with a flurry of interest in skating (popular on Inverleith pond), sledging and skiing.

A mounted policeman escorts the Hearts' team bus along Princes Street after their Scottish Cup win in April 1956.

In 1955 Hibs became the first British team to enter a European competition. In the first round of the European Cup they were drawn against German champions Rot Weiss. Here, in the second leg, Jimmy Mulkerrin of Hibs has a shot blocked by Vorderbaumen and Wewers. The game ended 1-1 after Hibs had won the first game in Essen 4-0.

The Famous Five

In 1949 Hibs played what seemed an unremarkable friendly match against Nithsdale Wanderers, but it would prove to be a momentous occasion in the club's history. It was then that a group of players that would go on to be dubbed 'The Famous Five' played together for the first time.

The combination of Gordon Smith, Bobby Johnstone, Lawrie Reilly, Eddie Turnbull and Willie Ormond produced eight goals that day and they would go on to become one of the most feared forward lines in the country.

Though Hibs ended the 1949/50 season without a trophy, it was clear they were on the verge of something special and in 1950/51, the team realised their full potential as they won the championship by ten points and, with the Famous Five continuing to terrorise defences, the team retained their crown the following season.

Still idolised to this day by Hibs supporters, a stand at Easter Road stadium is named in their honour.

Bobby Johnstone

Lawrie Reilly

Willie Ormond

Gordon Smith

Eddie Turnbull

The Terrible Trio

In September 1948 Willie Bauld made his debut for Hearts in a League Cup tie against the holders, East Fife, scoring a hat-trick in a 6-1 thrashing. More importantly, the game marked the start of a partnership that would come to be known as 'The Terrible Trio' with Bauld, Jimmy Wardhaugh and Alfie Conn all featuring together for the first time. In the next decade the players would go on to score more than 500 goals for Hearts.

During the Fifties, Hearts never finished outside the top four in the League, winning the championship in 1957/58 and 1959/60 and winning the League Cup in 1954/55, 1958/59 and 1959/60 as well as the Scottish Cup in 1955/56.

Alfie Conn

Jimmy Wardhaugh

Willie Bauld

Clyde v Hibs Scottish Cup final at Hampden in April 1958. Clyde keeper McCulloch saves Joe Baker's shot.

Hibs legend Lawrie Reilly scores against Dundee in March 1950, after getting past keeper Billy Brown. In fact, the keeper, by pulling Reilly back, caught the ball on the line, but the linesman declared it was over. The final score was a 4-2 win for Hibs.

Top left: Miss Lockhart Cowan drives off the first tee at Ingliston during the Edinburgh Ladies' Inter-Club Tournament in 1958. In that year the Ingliston estate was acquired by the Royal Highland and Agricultural Society of Scotland as a permanent venue for the Royal Highland Show.

Top right: South African golfer Gary Player holds the Claret Jug after winning the 1959 Open Championship at Muirfield, East Lothian.

Above: A view from the clubhouse at Muirfield Golf Course, East Lothian during the 1952 Curtis Cup match between Great Britain and the USA. Great Britain won by 5 matches to 4, winning the cup for the first time.

Tossing the caber at the 1953 City of Edinburgh Highland Games at Murrayfield Stadium.

Boating enthusiasts launching a boat down the slipway at Cramond in 1956.

Well-dressed football fans at Easter Road watch Hibs play against Falkirk in 1958.

Spectators and bookmakers at Musselburgh watch the finish of the 1952 Edinburgh Spring Handicap, won by Highland Clan.

Cars racing during Edinburgh's first ever stock car race meeting held at Meadowbank.

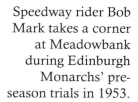

Speedway rider Bob Mark takes a corner at Meadowbank during Edinburgh Monarchs' pre-season trials in 1953.

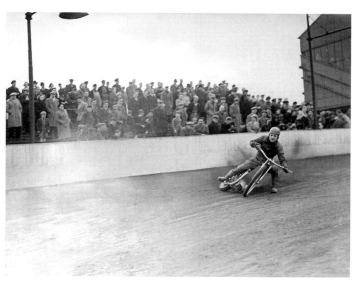

These riders are about to crash during a cycle speedway match between Edinburgh Falcons and Manchester Select at Pilrig Park, Leith.

Meadowlark Lemon scores during a basketball exhibition match at Murrayfield Ice Rink, between the Harlem Globetrotters and the Texas Cowboys. He played the fourth quarter wearing a kilt!

WELCOME HOME JACKIE BROWN

Empire Games Boxing Gold Medalist Jackie Brown is welcomed home to Lyne Street, Edinburgh.

Former boxer turned coach Tommy Bruce playfully spars with Bobby Donald at Edinburgh's Sparta Boxing Club.

Christy Elliot kicks Scotland's points in a 3-3 draw in the
1958 Calcutta Cup match against England at Murrayfield.

A desperate tackle by a white-shirted Scotland player during their
12-8 victory over Australia at Murrayfield in February 1958.

USA and Canadian Women curling tourists played an Edinburgh team at Haymarket Ice Rink. Mrs T G Devitt gets close to the action and guides the stone in while Mrs Andy Grant, Mrs Jane Squire and Miss L Squires look on.

Ski-jumping came to the Braid Hills in Edinburgh in 1951. Fifty-five tons of snow were brought from Norway and a temporary jump constructed. Crowds of over 10,000 people gathered to watch on the two days of competition.

Hundreds of people take advantage of the winter weather to go skating on Inverleith Pond.

Winter sports on the Braid Hills as heavy snow in Edinburgh in 1958 made ideal conditions for sledging and skiing.

Conclusion

Looking at an aerial view of Edinburgh in the 1950s, what is remarkable is how little it has changed over nearly 60 years.

That vast swathes of this vibrant capital city appear to have remained constant during a period of unprecedented change in society is pretty startling, yet so much seems familiar: the Union Canal still is host to rowers; walkers and cyclists continue to traverse along its banks, although the North British Rubber Company has since been demolished; Dean Village is still beautiful; in Princes Street Gardens, visitors still admire the latest reincarnation of the same floral clock, children still feed the pigeons and the public still flocks to the open air stage.

Along with its characteristic geography, most of the city's Old Town and New Town is unaltered. Roads such as George Street still seem to suffer the same parking pandemonium today as they clearly did in 1959. The streets are still as crowded with shoppers, but if you think Princes Street in August is mobbed nowadays, just look at the sea of people who assembled for the Gathering of the Clans, part of the Festival of Britain in 1951, surpassing anything seen in the largest of the most recent crop of Hogmanay crowds. The Royal Mile still is, as it was then, witness to stirring parades of pipers in their timeless uniforms. Parades of a different sort still take place in Edinburgh Zoo to this day, with the penguins still delighting generations of visitors.

Of course, certain areas have undergone radical transformation since the 1950s. Leith Fort, which had previously housed prisoners of the Napoleonic Wars, was closed in 1955. The poor condition of many slums in St Leonards and Greenside Row off Leith Street resulted in demolition. St James Square and George Square have also changed dramatically. Indeed, both areas are still changing. The former will metamorphose with the planned redevelopment of the St James Centre; and the current reconstruction of Edinburgh University buildings is forecast to continue well into the 2010s.

In 1957, Lothian Road was developed to ease traffic congestion. The city suffered disruption while tram lines were removed from its streets. Fifty years later, a modicum of mayhem once more results from the re-introduction of trams.

Yes, what is remarkable is the constancy apparent over the decades and the realisation that some things really don't change.

LORAINE AFFLECK (INNES)
EDWARD AIRLIE
BOB AITKEN
FRANCIS ALEXANDER
TAM ALEXANDER
DEREK W ALLAN
RONALD ANDERSON
JANET ANDERSON
NAN ANDERSON
TO ANNE
GRAHAM AULD
TOM AULD
ANNA BACCIARELLI
THOMAS WANLESS BAILLIE
ELLA BARR
SANDRA BARRON
JOHN BELL
ROY BELL
AUNTY BETTY
KATE BEVERIDGE
SCOTT BILLETT
ROBERT C. BIRD (IN
MEMORIES OF THE 50s –
LILLIAN)
JOHN BISKUP
ISABELLA BISKUP
ROBERT BISSET
EUNICE BLACK
ADAM BLACK
JANET BODY
LORNA MARION BRUCE
NEE BOLTON
DEREK BOWMAN
ANNE BRECHIN
FRED BRIEN
KEN BROTHERSTON
BILL BROWN
GEORGE BROWN
ELEANOR CLUNIE BROWN
MARGARET BROWNHILL
(WITH MEMORIES OF
HAPPY TIMES – BIRDIE)
ROBERT I BRUCE
TERENCE BURGOYNE
MR BURNETT
KEN BURNS
CHRISTOPHER ROBERTSON
BURNSIDE
JOAN LOUISE CAIRNS
GERALD CAMERON
FIONA MARY CAMERON
MARK CAMPBELL
ELIZABETH CAMPBELL
FRANCES CAMPBELL
NEIL CAMPBELL
MAT CAMPBELL
ELEANOR CAMPBELL

JUNE CAMPLIN
ROBERT CARR
ELISE CARR
RAYMOND CARSTAIRS
BETTY & LES CASTLE
ROBERT CAVEN
KRZYSZTOF CHUCHRA
MARINA CLEETON
GEORGE AND JEANETTE
CLUNIE
GEORGE COLEMAN
JOHN & JEAN COLLIE
GERRY COURTNEY
GEORGE COWLE
MAISIE AND DAVID CRAFT
GEORGE CURRENT
RICHARD S. DAKERS
SCOTT D. L. DAKERS
BETTY AND STANLEY
DAVIDSON
D. HUGH DAVIDSON
ALEX DAVIE
CHARLES DENNIS
KAREN DICKIE
DAVID DICKSON
MRS DICKSON
KEITH FRASER DICKSON
MARGARET DODDS
ALISDAIR DONALD
DONALD JOHN MORRISON
ELIZABETH DOUGLAS
JIM DOW
BETSY DRUMMOND
JOHN DRUMMOND
SHEENA DUNCAN
RAYMOND ELLIS
MARGARET MARSHALL
THOM ELLIS
DOUGLAS ELPHINSTONE
ERNIE
JIM FAIRHURST
ELIZABETH FERGUS
MRS. LESLEY FERGUSON
ROBERT SMITH FLINT
ELAINE FLYNN
FIONA FORBES
JIM FORREST
FRANCES
HAMISH FRASER
TOM FRASER
JIM FRENCH
WILLIAM DOUGLAS FREW
PATRICK GALLAGHER
PROF MICHAEL GARDNER
ELIZABETH GEBBIE
DOUGLAS GIBB
ANDREW & MANDY GIBB

MOIRA GIBBS
JOHN T GIBSON
MICHAEL GILBERT
RONALD GLASGOW
JOHN GLASGOW
PETER GLASGOW
GEORGE GLEN
JOHN GLEN
JOHN ALLEN GOODLET
JOAN GORDON
MR STEPHEN GORDON
KATRIONA GOWANS
MARGARET GRAHAM
JOHN WATT GRANT
JOHN & PAMELA GRANT-
WOOD
HELEN GREENLAW
ROBIN & CATH GRIERSON
JAMES C.L. GULLEN
GORDON HAMILTON
THOMAS WALLACE
HANRATTY
WILLIAM ARCHIBALD
HARKINS
ERNEST HARRIS
CAROLINE HENDERSON
MARION HENDERSON
MR J HOGARTH
THOMAS HOGG
ANNETTE HOGG
IRENE HOOD
JEAN HOPE
HELEN HOUSTON
MARGARET HOWIESON
– (WITH FONDEST
MEMORIES OF THE 50s –
LILLIAN)
STEVEN HUGHES
JANETTE HUGHSON
HAZEL HUNTER
JUNE HUNTER
PEGGY HUNTER
JIM INGLIS
MARGARET R IRVINE
MARY JACK
CYNTHIA MAGARET
JAMIESON (S.R.N. WESTERN
GENERAL INFIRMARY)
GRETA JOHNSTON
JAMES JOHNSTONE
RAYMOND DAVIDSON KAY
JOHN KERR
ANDREW KERR
VIOLET KERR
DOROTHY KERR
ELIZABETH KINGMAN
JIM KNIGHT

ERIC KNOTT
MR PHILIP KNOWLES
ROBERT H LAIDLAW
JIM AND CHRISTINE LAING
IRENE LANG
MRS HELEN MOIRA BURNS
LAWRIE
ENA LEARMONTH
ALEX LEITCH
BOB LESLIE
KAY LINDSAY
MARGARET LITTLEJOHN
DAVID A LYLE
RICHARD MABON
MARION MACDONALD
MARY SCOTT
MACFARLANE
ELEANAR MACK
ROBERT MACKENZIE
MARY MACLEAN
NEIL HUGH MACLEAN
DONALD MACMILLAN
GILLIAN MACPHERSON
JIM AND MARION
MRS ANNE MARTIN
THE MARTIN FAMILY
ERIC & IRENE MASON
EVELYNE MATHER
SHEENA MATHESON
STEWART MAYNE
MRS HELEN MCALISTER
LARRY MCALLISTER
HILDA MCCABE
ARCHIBALD MCCALL
BRIAN MCCARTHY
JOHN MCDONALD
JOHN GIBB & KAREN
MCDONALD
ARTHUR IAIN MCDONALD
GORDON MCDOUGALD
VERONICA MCGOWAN
JOHN MCINTOSH
SUSAN MCINTYRE
ROSALIND MCKENZIE
PATRICIA MCKNIGHT
THE MCLARENS
FLORENCE MCLEAN
EDITH MCMILLAN
MERION MCNAUGHTON
MARYANN E MCNEILL
IAN MCROBBIE
SARAH MCTERNAN
MURIEL MELVIN
DEWAR MELVIN
AMELIA & DEWAR MELVIN
ALAN MICHAEL
DAVID KAY MILLAR

SCOTT MILLER
KEITH F. MILLER
ANGUS K. MILLER
STANLEY WATT MILNE
JANET MILNES
JAMES MOFFAT
DR PETER MORRIS
DOUGLAS COLIN MOYES
JEAN MUIR
ANDREW MURRAY
STEWART MURRAY
NORMAN MURRAY
ROBIN MURRAY
ROBERT NEIL
JIM NICHOL
VERONICA NICOL
DAVID GORDON NISBET
SHARON AND PETER
NIVEN
OLIVE
RON OWEN
ARTHUR PARSONS
ROB AND PAT
ANDREW PAXTON
JEAN PENROSE
LORNA ELIZABETH
PERRISS
FRANCES PORTEOUS
MORNING SIDE MEDICAL
PRACTICE
JAMES QUINN
CHRISTINE REDDICK
JOAN REID
WILMA REID
BILL RENWICK
JO RICHARDS
CHRISTINE RICHARDSON
GORDON AND ELSIE
RICHARDSON
PETER RIDDLE
MR AND MRS ROBERT S
RILLEY
JOHN RITCHIE
WILLIAM ROBERTSON
BILL RODGER
ANNE RODGER
DAVID G. ROSE
JOHN ROSS
GAVIN ROSS
NORMAN RUSH
DOROTHY SAMSON
MARGARET SAWERS
GORDON SCOTT
CHRISTOPHER SENTIMAN
DONALD MCKENZIE
SHARP
IAN & SHEILA

ALAN SHIELS
NEIL G. SIMPSON
MARGARET SINCLAIR
C. SINCLAIR
ELIZABETH M. SINCLAIR
HUGH SKELDON
MARGARET & GORDON
SMART
WILLIAM ANDERSON
SMITH
ALICE ROSE SNEDDON
D G I STEARS
MOYRA STEWART
ALASTAIR STEWART
IAN WILLIAM STEWART
IRENE STODDART
JOHN STURROCK
JAMES SUMMERS
R W SUTHERLAND
ARCHIE SYME
ERIC TAYLOR
DAVID TERRACE
DAVID THOMSON
ALEX & DOROTHY
THOMSON
KATH THORBURN
WILLIAM THORBURN
MARY TITTERINGTON
MARTIN TODD (WITH
FONDEST MEMORIES OF
THE 50s – LILLIAN)
AGNES TRAINER
MAUREEN URBAN
GEORGE VALLANCE
CHARLES WARDELL
DOREEN WARWICK
MARGARET WATSON
THELMA WATSON
MRS SUSAN D. WAUGH
STEVE WEBB
CHRISTINA E WEBSTER
JANET WEIR
KEVIN PETER WEIR
DOUGLAS WIGHT
MICHAEL & SANDRA
WILKINSON
D. KAY WILLIAM
PAMELA ROSEMARY
WILLIAMS
MAY WILSON
LEN WILSON
JERRY WILSON
GEORGE BELL WILSON
JEFF & SHEILA WILSON
DANIEL DEWAR WISHART
ROBERT WRIGHT
EDWIN WRIGHT

Fabulous Historic Memorabilia from

THE SCOTSMAN

Visit The Scotsman's Photos Today website for our fabulous collection of historic photographs dating back as far as the 1930s!

You'll find many Old Edinburgh photographs, as well as images capturing famous historical moments. Take a look down memory lane and remind yourself of times gone by...

For more details or to order, call: 0131 620 8278, or buy online at www.photogallery.scotsman.com

Hold the front page..!
A unique gift for any special occasion

The Scotsman's Front Page gift service makes an excellent unique gift for friends or family and is perfect for special birthdays or anniversaries, or lovely for decoration in any home or office.

You can order the front page from the day someone was born, or on the day of a special historic event dating right back to 1817!

As well as a unique & thoughtful keepsake for Scots living at home or abroad, the Scotsman Front Page also makes a great gift for historians or academic enthusiasts who want to mark and display significant moments in history (please keep in mind the event would usually hit the headlines the day after the date of the event).

To make an enquiry or to order your copy now, call 0131 620 8280, or visit our website: www.shop.scotsman.com/frontpage

Edinburgh Evening News Living Memories Calendar

Few cities in the world can boast the enduring allure of Edinburgh. Over the decades, The Edinburgh Evening News has reported and recorded the changes that have taken place in our city. The images captured in our calendar, from the newspaper's vast collection of photographs, offer a unique portrait of the city's changing face.

Order your Edinburgh Evening News Living Memories Calendar today.

Call our order-line on 0131 620 8755 (quoting Ref: Book) or visit our website: www.scotsman-calendar.com

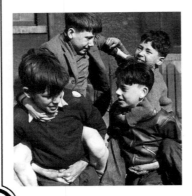